I Was A Teenage Jekyll and Hyde

Books and lyrics by Randall Lewton

Music by
Peter Miller

Samuel French – London
New York – Sydney – Toronto – Hollywood

ISBN 978 0 573 18009 5

Please see page iv for further copyright information

CHARACTERS

Ricky Fantasy, a teenage heart-throb
Sylvester Jekyll, a downtrodden youth
Hyde, a superboy
Eustace Crucible, crazed chemistry teacher
Miss Wrenplacket, a clueless music teacher
Angela
Gail
Denise
Chris } unhappy children
Eddie
Barry
Keith
Inspector Ticket, of Scotland Yard
Slasher, your nightmares made flesh
Kid Mozart
Billy Vandal } the band
Everton Cool
Bert Jekyll
Annie Jekyll } fond parents
Ricky's Fan Club
Hyde's Harem
Muggers and Thugs
Pupils
An Old Lady
A Blind Man
Little Girl

COPYRIGHT INFORMATION

I Was A Teenage Jekyll And Hyde was first presented at Alsop Comprehensive School, Liverpool on 14th July 1981 with the following cast:

Ricky Fantasy	Paul Macmillan
Sylvester Jekyll	David Foster
Hyde	Stephen Kinley
Eustace Crucible	Ed. Franklin
Miss Wrenplacket	Jackie Edge
Angela	Michelle Tansley
Gail	Hellene Murphy
Denise	Lorraine Carter
Chris	Derek Hignett
Eddie	Martin Handley
Keith	Paul Kinley
Inspector Ticket	Fred Schober
Slasher	Alex Mahoney
	Andy McGowan
Bert Jekyll	Eric Tucker
Annie Jekyll	Maureen Woods

and

Tim Evans	Nichola Marr	Andrew Holmes
Andy Billinge	Julie Ross	David Holme
Keith Bristow	Bernie Graham	Gary Place
Philip Stedman	Cathy Freckleton	Andrew Freeman
Gillian Kirkham	Karen Grainger	Lee Alderdice
Jackie Marshall	Graham Carlin	Mark Jenkins
Jackie Everett		

Also involved were:

Colyn Vaughan	Harry Weatherley	Gary Leahy
Alan Pevely	Peter Mitchell	Brian Hampson
Chris Dawson	Ian Muir	Philip Jones
Alice Pedder	Jonathan Somerville	
Steve Toms	John Charnock	
Anthony Butler	Michael Dillon	
Graham Minton	Gary Shipton	
Richard Sadler	Douglas Cashin	
John Owen	Sheila Spiers	
Roy Hedges	Alan Hemmings	

MUSICAL NUMBERS

1. **Have We Got A Story** — Ricky and his Fan Club
2. **Happiness** (and reprise) — Sylvester
3. **Let's Skit Together** — Ricky and band
4. **Wanna Girl** — Sylvester, Eddie, Chris
   Happiness (reprise)
5. **Wanna Boy** — Gail, Denise
6. **Superboy-Superstar** — Crucible
7. **How Do You Feel?** — Crucible, Sylvester, Hyde
8. **One Day** — Miss Wrenplacket, Angela
9. **Love, Love, Nothing But Love** — Hyde and band
10. **All The Best Days Of My Life** — Hyde

11. **Out On The Beat** — Ticket
12. **Points Of View** — Crucible, Angela, Ticket, Hyde, Bert, Annie
13. **Problem Page** — Chris, Eddie, Gail, Denise, Girls
14. **I Rule** — Hyde
15. **Society** — Ricky and muggers
    One Day (reprise) — Miss Wrenplacket
16. **Science Can Be Fun** — Crucible
17. **Shakespeare — No Rubbish** — Hyde and band
18. **It's My Life** — Sylvester and Hyde
19. **Be Yourself** — Company

PRODUCTION NOTES

Staging

The play can easily be performed on any kind of stage or in any space, although it is essential to have some kind of raised area behind the acting area as a "stage" for the band. A platform projecting out into the audience is useful for separation in the scenes where two pieces of action are taking place simultaneously, for speeding up scene changes and to make the dialogues between Ricky, Inspector Ticket and the Audience more "intimate". The ground plan shows how our stage looked.

Cast

It will be clear from the script that some of the cast have to be able to sing well. The rest only have to be able to sing loudly! Enthusiasm will make up for lack of musical talent in the Chorus. Have as many people in the Chorus as will fit on your stage. Why wait? Have your nervous breakdown *this* year. It is not essential, but probably better, to use adults for the adult parts. This should be no problem in a school production. You will probably be trampled in the rush of staff anxious to make fools of themselves. Staff involvement also sells tickets.

Scenery

No "sets" as such are required. The bare stage with the band permanently set up on a rear platform is used for the Youth Club and some other scenes. Other locations are suggested by items of furniture and light free-standing items of scenery (see Furniture and Property List).

Sylvester's house	– Armchair, TV, ironing board, perhaps a "window" gobo (see Equipment and Effects)
Chemistry Laboratory	– the lab. bench, chairs/stools, Slasher's trunk, a free-standing doorway is useful
The School Library	– tables, chairs, SILENCE sign (our letters were attached to a stage curtain track with fishing line and bulldog clips so that they could easily be pulled down when required)
Hyde's pad	– Sofa, screen of some kind
Back alley	– Dustbins, crates, piles of rubbish, a free-standing section of wall, perhaps a "fire escape" gobo

Flats at the sides of our stage were painted matt black and fitted with hooks on which all the chairs (brightly painted) were hung when not in use. A cyclorama is useful for projected disco effects in the youth club scenes. If you don't have one, paint some flats white.

Equipment and Effects

The laboratory bench

It is much easier to deal with if it is on wheels: cover it with lab. equipment, preferably brightly coloured. The top of the bench must have holes for feeding creatures, etc. (see p. 16). There must be sufficient space inside/behind it to conceal Hyde and/or Jekyll.

In Act Two it has to be wired up for the "Science Can Be Fun" number. Smoke guns, maroons and many kinds of pyrotechnics are available from theatrical suppliers (see "Amateur Stage" or Yellow Pages). Make this number as spectacular as your budget will allow. A *loud* bang at the end is essential. No anticlimactic "pops" please.

N.B. Pyrotechnics are fun but do be careful. Follow the manufacturers' instructions and keep all non-essential actors and stage staff well out of the way. The equipment should, of course, be in the charge of a responsible *adult*.

Lights

The youth club scenes are greatly enhanced by the use of disco and/or strobe lights. The strobe is also useful for the "transformations" and the violent moments, especially in the back alley scene.

A follow spot is a great help, in fact almost essential at the start of the second act. With a set of coloured filters its versatility will make it well worth the expense of hiring.

Consider, also, the use of gobos (metal cut-outs which fit into profile spots so that a shape is projected onto a wall or floor). They are available from theatrical suppliers in a wide variety of designs (windows, city lights, signs, fire escapes) or make your own. They are cheap and effective ways of suggesting a scene.

Sound

You will need *good* sound equipment. We used the band for about half the songs, the others being accompanied with piano only. When the band do play, the singers will need microphones, some hand-held and others strategically placed on the stage. Seek the advice of someone who understands the equipment and give the singers time to rehearse with it. Poor, distorted, incoherent sound will irritate your audience beyond measure and they won't be able to hear the lyrics. When hiring equipment, remember that you get what you pay for.

RANDALL LEWTON AND PETER MILLER

ACT ONE

The play opens in darkness. A drum roll is heard, followed by a taped voice

Voice Ladies and gentlemen, will you please welcome—Ricky Fantasy!

Ricky Fantasy, dressed in a ridiculous flashy stage suit, runs forward. A spotlight picks him out. Taped screams, cheers and applause accompany his entrance

Girls rush on from all sides, screaming. They carry posters and banners with Ricky's name and photograph on them, and everyone wears a Ricky badge

The Girls wave and reach out towards Ricky during his next speech

Ricky Thank you. Thank you. Good evening. How are you? (*He looks around at the Audience*) Now let me see. Is there anybody here tonight who's unhappy? (*Pointing*) Yes, over there. Looks miserable. Is there anybody here tonight who's always getting picked on? Yes, over there. Who picks on you? Really? Is there anybody here tonight whose parents don't understand them? Yes here   and there   Lot of those. Is there anybody here tonight who'd like to get his own back on the bullies, on the sneaks   on the teachers? All over the place. Is there anybody who'd like to be irresistible to members of the opposite sex? Gentleman down here says he already is. Well all of you—you've all come to the right place because tonight we've got the story for you.

1. Have We Got A Story

(*singing*) If your average score is zero
                Have we got a story
                If you'd rather be a hero
                Have we got a story,
                If you're longing to do what
                You've seen the others do
                Have we got a story for you!

(*speaking*) Tell them what we've got for them, girls.

Girls   We've got jokes that'll tickle your ribs
                We've made up and adjusted our wigs
                Learned our lines and rehearsed our ad-libs
                And we're here to let you know
                It's gonna be quite a show

Ricky   If it's supremacy you're seeking
Girls   Have we got a story

Ricky	For every seven stone weakling
Girls	Have we got a story
Ricky	If you've been waiting all your life
	To see your dreams come true
All	Have we got a story for you

There is a horrifying scream

The lights dim

> *Eustace Crucible, the crazed chemistry teacher, enters dragging a huge seemingly heavy, trunk*

A green spot picks Eustace out

> *The lid of the trunk begins to rise and Crucible fights to hold it down*

Ricky (*speaking*) Yeah   there are a few creepy bits too.

> *Crucible exits*

Lights return to previous level

> We've got songs you'll be whistling for years
> We'll have scenes that will move you to tears
> Poetry that can rival King Lear's
> We've great actors in each part
> Supreme dramatic art

Girls	We've a dance worthy of the ballet
	(Rehearsed it the first time yesterday)
Ricky	But we won't let that get in our way
Girls	We've a transformation scene
Ricky	And most of the jokes are clean

All	If your average score is zero
	Have we got a story
	And if you'd rather be a hero
	Have we got a story
	If you've been waiting all your life
	To see your dreams come true
	Have we got a story
	A shocking rocking story
	Have we got a story for you
	Have we got a story for you
	A shocking rocking rocking shocking story for you

During the final chorus the Girls bring on a desk piled high with books, a schoolbag, a chair and finally, as if he were another piece of furniture, they carry on Sylvester Jekyll, a downtrodden youth, and sit him at the desk

As the song ends the Girls dance off

Ricky (*quoting*) "Those that can pity here

May, if they think it well, let fall a tear
The subject will deserve it."

Whenever he is quoting, Ricky has an elevated "great acting" tone of voice

(*In a normal voice*) Shakespeare—no rubbish. "The subject will deserve it." That's the subject there. That, believe it or not, is the hero of our story. Name of Sylvester. Only son of Mr and Mrs Herbert Jekyll. Sylvester is not a happy lad. He has a lot of problems. Being called Sylvester is the least of them. At the moment he's a little depressed.

Sylvester enters figures furiously on a pocket calculator. He pushes buttons and writes frenziedly. He finally closes the book

Sylvester At last—finished the French. That only leaves   (*He pulls about ten more books out of his bag*)   Maths, History, Physics, Chemistry and Biology. It'll take me all night. Everyone else is out playing football. (*He slumps over his books*)

Music 2 begins quietly. Sylvester lifts his head and sings

2. Happiness

(*Singing*) Other kids are happy
Why them and why not me?
The story of my life has been
A tale of misery

(*Speaking*) But what's the use of complaining?

Happiness, I can do without it
Who wants it? Who needs it anyway?
Happiness, I don't think about it
As I work here like a slave from day to day
Sometimes imagination brings before my eyes
A place where the word "Homework" no one knows
Then I feel twice as miserable and realize
It's better just to do without
It's better not to think about
Impossible dream worlds like those

Sylvester trudges off

The Girls remove the desk and chair

The Music Class assembles as Ricky speaks

Ricky You see, Sylvester wasn't exactly brilliant. Bottom of the class in every lesson. Like music. I mean, "If music be the food of love   " I told you, Shakespeare—no rubbish. "If music be the food of love   ", Sylvester was on a crash diet.

Ricky exits

The lights come up to reveal the Music Class. Miss Wrenplacket stands in front

*of a class of boys and girls arranged in rebellious positions and all chewing gum
ostentatiously. She is bespectacled with her hair in a bun and wearing dull,
baggy clothes*

*A tape of classical music is playing. Miss Wrenplacket is in another world,
rapturously conducting the unseen orchestra. Her class is bored. The music ends*

Miss Wrenplacket (*without looking at the class*) In my opinion that is one of
the most exciting pieces of music ever written. (*She turns and looks at the
class. Immediately she becomes flustered*) Er   what did you think about
it?

There is silence

Anybody?

There is silence

Er   Keith, what did you think?
Keith Don't know.
Miss Wrenplacket Well you must have formed some kind of opinion. Did
you like it?
Keith Not a lot.
Miss Wrenplacket Did anybody like it?

There is silence

What about you, Barry? You're a musician.
Keith No he's not. He's a drummer. (*He laughs*)

There is general laughter

Barry You're only jealous 'cos we won't have you in the band.
Miss Wrenplacket All right. All right.
Keith Get away. I've heard your band. It should be.
Barry What?
Keith Banned!
Girl 1 Leave him alone. They're all right.
Keith They're all right if you're deaf.
Barry Listen. If you don't shut up, I'll be drumming on your head.
Keith You wanna try?

Barry and Keith get up

Miss Wrenplacket Sit down. Stop it!

The class all start to shout encouragement

Keith! Barry!

Keith and Barry move towards each other

Barry You think you're really clever, don't you?
Keith Compared to you, yeah.

Keith and Barry square up. The class shouts louder

Miss Wrenplacket (*helplessly*) Please   stop   sit down.

As the fight is about to begin there is a clap of thunder

The door flies open and Eustace Crucible, more crazed than usual, walks in

The class screams and then there is total silence. Crucible glares at the class, marches past them and turns and snarls at them. The class shrink back. Crucible turns away from them towards Miss Wrenplacket. The class leans forward again. He turns swiftly towards them. They shrink back again. He turns away

Crucible Is everything all right, Miss Wrenplacket?

Miss Wrenplacket looks embarrassed and fiddles with her hair and smooths her dress

Miss Wrenplacket Yes. Yes. Thank you, Mr Crucible. I'm afraid our discussion was getting a bit lively. I hope we didn't disturb you. (*She laughs nervously*)

Crucible (*taking her to one side*) Listen to the voice of experience, Miss Wrenplacket.

Crucible glares at the class. They wince

You need a firm hand. (*He shows her his fist*) A firm hand.

Crucible takes Miss Wrenplacket's hand and forms it into a fist. She is visibly thrilled

There is a horrible moaning sound offstage

Crucible goes to the door

(*Shouting*) Quiet! (*To the class*) I am in the next room. I do not wish to be disturbed.

Crucible marches out

Miss Wrenplacket stands gazing at her clenched fist

Sylvester enters and goes over to the class

There is an empty seat next to Keith on which is Keith's schoolbag. Sylvester puts the bag on the floor and sits on the seat. Keith notices this, taps Sylvester, and points at the bag. Sylvester gets up, puts the bag back on the chair and sits on the floor. Miss Wrenplacket comes out of her dream

Miss Wrenplacket A firm hand. Yes. Right, Sylvester, give out these books please. (*She hands him a pile of books*)

Sylvester takes the books and starts to give them out. Keith knocks the pile from his hands

Now we've been practising this for weeks now. Let's see if we can do it with a little *enthusiasm*, shall we? Ready   one, two, three, four.

Each member of the class produces an instrument and starts to play the "1812 Overture" perfectly (taped) Miss Wrenplacket taps to stop them. They stop very suddenly except for Sylvester who is scraping away horribly at a violin. Miss Wrenplacket walks over to him, takes away the violin and gives him a tambourine. He holds it up. She turns away. He drops it

Miss Wrenplacket Ready. Carrying on   one, two, three, four.

The music plays again. Sylvester stands motionless, waiting for his moment. When it comes and all the others stop, he just stands there. They all stare at him. He wakes up, realizes, smashes the tambourine and puts his hand through it

Keith He's hopeless.

2a. Happiness (reprise)

Class	*(together)*	You're hopeless, Sylvester
Miss Wrenplacket		And at music you are a flop
		Your best subject is failure
		That's where you come out on top
Angela *(aside)*		Free yourself, accept yourself
		Be yourself, respect yourself
		Don't feel sorry for yourself
		Ignore the rest, be more yourself

Angela looks lovingly at Sylvester No one notices

  The class, except Sylvester and Angela, leaves

  Ricky returns

  The band enter and take up their positions and begin to play

  Dancers enter and fill the stage. Chris, Keith, his girlfriend and Eddie are among them

Ricky All that Mozart stuff's not really my kind of music. I prefer something a bit more exciting, you know What's that? "My music playing far off." Like I said   Shakespeare no rubbish. This is a good band. Plays at the youth club at school. The singer's terrific. Great voice. Great looks.

He starts to go, but looks back

By the way – that's me.

The Lights come up to reveal the Youth Club. Ricky joins the band

3. Let's Skit Together

(Singing)   We like to bear malice
               And call people names
               To hurt and embarrass
               Our principal aims
               We ain't ashamed of it
               We freely can admit
               It's cruel but we love it

> Yeah we love to
> we love to
> we love to
>   skit!

All   Hey baby, let's skit together
                   Hey baby, let's skit it right
                   Hey baby, let's skit together
                   Hey baby, let's skit tonight

The music stops abruptly. Everyone "freezes" except Girl 1 and Girl 2

Girl 1 Who, him?
Girl 2 Yeah, the singer.
Girl 1 Never
Girl 2 He is.
Girl 1 In our school?
Girl 2 Yeah.
Girl 1 I've never heard of anyone called Ricky Fantasy.
Girl 2 That's only like his stage name.
Girl 1 What's his real name then?
Girl 2 Bernard Clapfish.

Everyone "unfreezes" and the action continues

Ricky (*singing*)   Skit, skit, skit
                        It makes us look good
                        Skit, skit, skit
                        'Cos we've understood
                        Skit, skit, skit
                        That while you condemn
                        Skit, skit, skit, skit
                        You're better than them
                        Skit, skit, skit
                        Your girl or your mate
                        Skit, skit, skit
                        It makes you feel great
                        Skit, skit, skit
                        Your teacher, your boss
                        Skit, skit, skit
                        When his back's turned of course.

Everyone "freezes" except Chris and Sylvester

Chris Me sister told me.
Sylvester (*disbelievingly*) Yeah.
Chris Honest. She fancies yer She told me sister and me sister told me.
Sylvester What's her name?
Chris I told yer. Angela. Go and ask her to dance.
Sylvester *I* can't dance, can I?
Chris You can have a go. It doesn't matter.

Sylvester Naw.
Chris Oh I give up. You're hopeless. (*He walks away*)

Sylvester sits down

The action continues

Ricky (*singing*)   Hey baby, let's skit together
                             Hey baby, let's skit it right
                             Hey baby, let's skit together
                             Hey baby, let's skit tonight

Everyone "freezes" except Angela and Sylvester

Angela sits next to Sylvester

Angela D'you like the band?
Sylvester Yeah   good   yeah.

There is a pause

Angela Been dancing have you?
Sylvester Er   no   not yet.

There is a pause

Angela No I haven't either.
Sylvester No?

There is a pause

Angela No   not yet.
Sylvester Plenty of time.

There is a pause

Angela I

There is a pause

Sylvester What?
Angela Nothing.

The action continues again

Ricky (*singing*)   Skit, skit, skit
                             It makes us look good
                             Skit, skit, skit
                             'Cos we've understood
                             Skit, skit, skit
                             That while you condemn
                             Skit, skit, skit
                             You're better than them

Everyone "freezes" except Chris and Sylvester

Chris sits down on the other side of Sylvester

Chris That's her
Sylvester Who?
Chris Angela. Sitting next to you.

Sylvester takes a sly look. Angela pretends not to notice

Ask her to dance.
Sylvester I can't.
Chris It's easy. You just open your mouth and *ask* her.
Sylvester But I *can't* dance.
Chris That's not stopping anyone else.
Sylvester I'd make a fool of myself.
Chris Ah you're just chicken.

The action continues. Sylvester takes several deep breaths. Keith and his girlfriend sit next to Angela

Angela leaves in despair

Ricky (*singing*)   Skit, skit, skit
                          Your girl or your mate
                          Skit, skit, skit
                          It makes you feel great
                          Skit, skit, skit
                          Your teacher, your boss
                          Skit, skit, skit
                          When his back's turned of course

Everyone "freezes"

Sylvester, with a determined look and with tightly closed eyes, reaches out and grabs what he thinks is Angela's wrist. Actually he gets hold of Keith's girlfriend. He pulls her to the dancing area

Sylvester Dance!

Keith walks over to where Sylvester is dancing, not having noticed his mistake. Sylvester sees Keith, realizes and stops dancing. Keith glares at him

All (*singing*)   Hey baby, let's skit together
                         Hey baby, let's skit it right
                         Hey baby, let's skit together
                         Hey baby, let's skit tonight

Everybody gathers round and laughs at Sylvester The laughter is amplified and distorted on tape

                         You're hopeless, Sylvester
                         As a dancer you are a flop
                         Your best subject is failure
                         That's where you come out on top.

Sylvester leaves in a hurry

The others pair off and leave

Chris and Eddie remain on stage

Eddie What am I doing wrong? Look at me.
Chris Do I have to?
Eddie No. Let's be honest. Look at me.
Chris Well   what?
Eddie Am I or am I not fantastically good looking?
Chris Er
Eddie Exactly. And am I or am I not looking cool in this gear?
Chris Well
Eddie You're right, I am. And did I or did I not have a bath and wash me soft
    and silky hair before I came out tonight?
Chris Did yer?
Eddie Correct. So will you please answer me one question?
Chris What's that?
Eddie Why am I standing here talking to you? Why am I not walking home
    with the young lady of my choice, stopping off at the park on the way in
    order to get to know her better.
Chris Know what you mean, Eddie.
Eddie I mean, I can't understand it. You're almost as magnetically attractive
    as I am meself. And look at us.

Sylvester returns

And here's another. Just saying, Sylvester, can't understand why we seem
to have this difficulty.
Sylvester I can.
Eddie Oh really?
Chris Go on then. Why?
Sylvester Well, you're skinny with bad breath, he's covered in pimples and
    spots and his nose is always running and I'm too scared to talk to them.
Eddie Well what do they want – perfection? It's not as if I'm demanding a
    beauty queen. I'll settle for anything.
Chris Makes no difference in the dark.

They all laugh

4. Wanna Girl

Eddie } (*together*) **Chris** }	What's the matter with you girls? Why can't you all see? What's the matter with these guys? What's the matter with me?
Eddie	When I was little I had a toy gun
Chris	When I was little Toy soldiers were fun
Sylvester	And when I was thirteen I still loved my teddy bear

All   But now we all want someone
                                With soft skin, big (*he gestures*), long hair

*Eddie sings the Chorus whilst Sylvester and Chris "Oooh" and "Aaah" as
backing*

	Chorus	*Backing*
Eddie	Wanna girl	Feeling bad,
	A hand to hold	I'm so sad,
	Wanna girl	So alone,
	'Fore I'm too old	For my own.
	Wanna girl	
	Two lips to kiss	
	Wanna girl	
	Can't live like this	

Chris   At our age it's a pity
                                To be left on the shelf
                                We're three good-looking fellers
                                So come on girls help yourself

Sylvester ⎱ (*together*)   Chris may be skinny
Eddie ⎰   But what's wrong with that
                                His body is thin
                                It's his head that is fat
                                A new brand of toothpaste
                                Will cure his stinking breath
                                If not his jokes, his fingers
                                Girls will tickle you to death

Chris sings the Chorus as a solo whilst Eddie and Sylvester provide the backing

Eddie   I need someone to love me
                                I can't do it by myself
                                Don't you know teenage frustration
                                Can be hazardous to health?

Sylvester ⎱ (*together*)   What's wrong with Eddie
Chris ⎰   Apart from the spots
                                The grease on his face
                                The holes in his socks?
                                A packet of Kleenex
                                Will cure his runny nose
Eddie   And all my moving parts are
                                Smoothly working   so

Eddie sings the Chorus as a solo, Chris and Sylvester backing him

Sylvester   Give generously girls
                                It's in a good cause

It's your lucky day girls
Come and get me, I'm yours

Sylvester sings the Chorus, with Eddie and Chris backing him

Sylvester, Eddie and Chris leave

Ricky returns, now dressed in ordinary clothes. Whilst he is speaking the Jekylls' home is set

Ricky Girls weren't Sylvester's only problem. You see, being weak and feeble, he has a lot of trouble with the school bully, a nasty character, a very nasty character.

He starts to go but turns back

By the way—that's me. (*He moves to the side of the stage*)

The Lights come up to reveal Sylvester's home. Bert Jekyll is sitting with his feet up watching television. He has a can of beer in one hand and a cigarette in the other He is scratching himself. Annie Jekyll is ironing

Annie What time is it, Bert?

There is no reply

Bert. What time is it?
Bert Shaddup. Don't know.
Annie Well it must be getting late. Isn't it time Sylvester was in?
Bert Pah! Sylvester.
Annie Isn't it time he was in?
Bert Don't know. Shaddup.

Sylvester enters at the opposite side of the stage

Ricky goes to meet Sylvester

Ricky Ey lad, you got any money? Lend us ten p.
Sylvester I've got none.
Ricky Don't believe yer.
Sylvester (*holding out his pocket linings*) You can search me if you like.
Ricky Well you can sponsor me then. (*He waves a form*)
Sylvester What is it?
Ricky We're having a sponsored boogie.
Sylvester A sponsored *boogie*?
Ricky Yeah. Just sign here.
Sylvester What's the money for?
Ricky It's for the band like.
Sylvester I'm not giving money to your band.
Ricky Ah now, Sylvester, don't be tight-fisted. Just sign it.
Sylvester (*backing away*) No.

Ricky grabs him and twists his arm

Ricky Now I don't want to have to twist your arm. Just put your name down.

Sylvester All right. All right. Let go. (*He signs*)
Annie I hope he's all right. What time is it?
Bert Don't know. Shaddup.
Annie You hear these stories about what goes on at these youth clubs. He's very small for his age, isn't he Bert?
Bert Skinny little rat. Shaddup.
Ricky Thank you very much. Very generous.

Sylvester starts to go

Just a minute. Come here.

Sylvester returns

You've made a mistake. You've put down one p. I'll just change it to ten p. OK?
Sylvester I can't afford
Ricky You can't afford not to, can you Sylvester?
Sylvester No. OK.

Sylvester goes into his "home"

Ricky (*to the audience*) Well, he's so pathetic. He's asking to be bullied, isn't he? Little worm.

Ricky exits

Annie Where have you been?
Sylvester I was only
Bert Don't speak like that to your mother. Shaddup.
Sylvester I didn't   I was only
Annie You heard what your father said.
Sylvester But
Bert Do I have to take me belt off to you? Shaddup.
Sylvester No, I was just
Bert Don't you tell me "No"! (*He starts to get up*)
Sylvester I didn't mean
Annie Sylvester, why are you always like this?
Bert (*slumping down*) Ah look at yer. If I give you a belt, I'll probably put you in hospital. How a son of mine can be a shrivelled little runt like you I'll never know.
Annie You'll have to buck up you know, Sylvester.
Bert ⎫   You've been a great disappointment to your mother and
        ⎬ (*together*)   me.
Annie ⎭   You've been a great disappointment to your father and
                             me.

Sylvester moves forward, looking miserable

Bert and Annie leave

Strike the Jekylls' home

Music 2b starts

2b. Happiness (reprise)

Sylvester Happiness, I can do without it
Who needs it? Who wants it anyway?
Happiness, I don't think about it
When they scold and criticize me every day
Sometimes imagination brings before my eyes
A Mum and Dad who'd love me as I chose
Then I feel twice as miserable and realize
It's better just to do without
It's better not to think about
Impossible dream worlds like those

Sylvester trudges off

Gail makes a dramatic entrance, closely followed by Denise

Gail (*wailing*) Waaaaaaaaaaaaaaaaaaah!
Denise Hey, Gail. Shurrup.
Gail Waaaaaaaaaaaaaaaaaaah!
Denise He'll be back.
Gail Waaaaaaaaaaaaaaaaaaah!
Denise He was a creep anyway.

Gail stops crying suddenly

Gail Better than "that" you were going out with.

There is a pause

Denise (*wailing*) Waaaaaaaaaaaaaaaaaaah!
Gail What's the matter with us, Denise?
Denise There's nothing the matter with *me*.
Gail There's nothing the matter with me either.
Denise Well I wish somebody would tell them that.
Gail That's the fourth feller that's chucked me.
Denise And that's only this week.
Gail Waaaaaaaaaaaaaaaaaaah!
Denise I mean we do all the things they say, like, don't we?

There is a pause

Gail Who say?
Denise (*pulling out a magazine*) In here. Like this – "Boys – how their minds work."
Both Minds?
Denise Or here – "101 ways to get a boyfriend."
Gail Oh yeah. I've tried 99 of them.
Denise What about the other two?
Gail I'm not *that* desperate.
Denise I think I am. I mean it's not much to ask, is it? I don't want anything special. An ordinary one would do.

5. Wanna Boy

Gail	He needn't be tall
Denise	He needn't be dark
Gail	I wanna hold hands
	And walk in the park
Denise	He needn't be handsome
	Built like Superman
Both	Let's face it we'll be grateful
	To get anyone we can

Angela enters and stands listening to the last chorus

Wanna boy
A hand to hold
Wanna boy
'Fore I'm too old
Wanna boy
Two lips to kiss
Wanna boy
Can't live like this

After the song, there is a long pause. The three girls stare into the audience, then pull out handkerchiefs

Gail
Denise } *(together)* Waaaaaaaaaaaaaaaaaaaaaaaaaaaaaaaaaaah!
Angela

They run off

The Chemistry Lab. is set — a large bench covered in multi-coloured equipment, with a number of boxes and cages beneath it. Six stools are placed, facing the bench, and to one side is the large trunk seen earlier

Six pupils, including Sylvester and Angela, enter and sit on the stools

Crucible enters and begins talking

Sylvester is at one end of the bench, Angela at the other. All the pupils are writing furiously as Crucible dictates

Crucible   solution of potassium permanganate. Full stop.

The class executes a very loud full stop in perfect unison. Crucible glares at them

Question twenty-five. The oxide of metal X, having reacted with gas Y at a temperature of fifty degrees centigrade, is added to liquid Z. Carbon peroxide gas is given off. Is there any solution? And, if so, name it.

A bell rings. The class stirs. Crucible frowns and there is silence

I will have the answers to those tomorrow morning please. You may go.

The class leaves in silence, Sylvester leaving his book behind

Crucible waits until they have gone, then his mood changes and he cackles madly

At last. Four o'clock. Now I can get on with my real work.

He pulls out various boxes and cages, lifting the lids

Ah my creatures! How are you? Time for tea.

He brings out a tray with various items on it. He feeds a huge snake into the first box. Chomping sounds come from the box

You know it does me good to see something enjoying its food. (*He moves on to the next box*) How's your indigestion today? Better? Let's see.

He feeds a large photo of the Prime Minister into the box. Chomping, licking of lips and a belch come from the box

Good. Good. If you can stomach that, you can stomach anything.

He moves on. He holds up a flask of bubbling green liquid and pours a few drops into the next box

That's enough. You are on a diet you know.

There is a horrifying roar   A hairy hand comes out of the box and grabs the liquid. Slurping noises are heard, then the hand throws the glass out

Heh. Heh. Only kidding.

He slams the lid back on, pours liquids and looks busy

A few more hours and I will be famous. Fifteen years' work and today the reward. (*He comes forward holding a small test tube*) Fifteen years in this awful place. Fifteen years of horrible brats and infantile experiments. But now I have it – the culmination, the supreme scientific achievement, for which I shall be known throughout history. Fifteen years for this one small tube.

He drops the test tube. It smashes

Aaaaaaaaagh! But no, wait a minute. This is the wrong tube. Where are we?

There is a roar from the trunk. He hits it

Quiet, Slasher

He collects the right test tube from the bench

My superdrug. One sip of this and I will become a superman strong, brave, intelligent (*correcting himself*) *more* intelligent, irresistible to women. After fifteen years this is the moment I have been waiting for

He is about to take a sip but pauses

I know well that I risk death. For any drug that can so potently control and shake the very fortress of identity might by the very least scruple of an overdose utterly blot out that immaterial tabernacle which I look to it to change. Yes, what if it doesn't work? The effect could be fatal. What's the matter with me? It's a chance I must take. (*To the Audience*) Am I a man or a mouse?

Hopefully the Audience will respond with "a mouse"

You're right. I'm a mouse. What I need is a guinea pig.

He moves over to the trunk, the lid of which is slowly opening

I need someone on whom I can test the drug so that I may observe the effect. But who?

"Something" grabs Crucible and pulls him into the trunk. There are screams and an enormous struggle

There is a knock at the door

Sylvester enters and knocks again

Sylvester Excuse me. Mr Crucible. Mr Crucible. Anyone here? I left my book. The homework.

Sylvester moves in nervously and looks for the book. The trunk shakes violently and Crucible fights his way out. Sylvester screams. Roars and growls are heard. Crucible sits on the lid of the trunk

Crucible Ah, Jekyll, my boy.
Sylvester Sorry, sir   I   it was   I just   homework   my book.
Crucible Of course. Of course. That's quite all right. Here it is. (*Aside*) This one might make a good guinea pig. But I wonder if he is sufficiently hopeless.

Sylvester knocks over a flask, spilling liquid all over Crucible

Sylvester Sir   I'm sorry   let me   (*He mops up*)
Crucible Perfect! Jekyll?
Sylvester Yes, sir.
Crucible Jekyll, have you ever wanted   Have you ever wished
Sylvester What sir?
Crucible Have you ever wished that you were someone special? Have you ever wanted to be that little bit stronger, that little bit cleverer, that little bit better than all the rest?
Sylvester Which little bit do you mean, sir?
Crucible I have created, Jekyll, a drug so revolutionary, so exciting, that it will make me world-famous — and you too.
Sylvester Me? How?
Crucible Is there a cat in here?
Sylvester No, sir. It was me. I said, "Me? How?"
Crucible (*aside*) I think the boy's half-witted.
Sylvester How will it make me famous, sir?
Crucible I want you to be the first to try it.

Sylvester What kind of a drug is it?
Crucible This is your chance. Now take it.

6. Superboy—Superstar

One sip of this potion, you'll feel you're alive
Euphoric, athletic (*aside*) that's if you survive
It won't be much more than ten seconds until you
Are metamorphosed (if the shock doesn't kill you)

Chorus
Yes this, my lad
Will show a side of you you never knew you had
With this, my boy
Everything you've ever wanted you'll enjoy
With this, my son
A whole new way of life will have begun
With this, my friend
Your days of misery are at an end

Our rise to immortality
Will be spectacular
Soon you will be a superboy
And I'll be a superstar
Superboy Superstar
Do you think you're what they say

(*Speaking, to the accompanist*) Just a minute. Stop. Will you stop. That's
the wrong song. It's the wrong song! I know it's hard to keep awake but
make an effort *please*.

One drop of this liquid, you'll feel light in the head
Drop fears, faults, inhibitions (or maybe drop dead)
If the formula works, the whole world we'll astound
You'll be walking on air (or six feet underground)

The Chorus is repeated

Sylvester That sounds like the very thing I've been praying for Yes. I'll try it,
sir
Crucible Good boy. Good boy Here. Just copy this note first.
Sylvester What is it?
Crucible It's just in case anything goes wrong. It just says you've run away
from home. So your parents won't worry.
Sylvester Oh right. (*He copies it*)
Crucible (*aside*) The boy *is* half-witted!

Sylvester hands him the note

Good. Here you are.

He gives the tube to Sylvester who quickly drinks the contents

No. Just a sip. You stupid boy. You've taken the lot!
Sylvester Oh! (*He clutches himself*)
Crucible What's the matter? How do you feel?

7. How Do You Feel?

Sylvester   Strange,
                       I feel strange!
                       Pain
                       Oh the pain

He doubles up in agony

Crucible (*taking out a notebook*)
                       Give me the details
                       Of your ordeal
                       Try to describe it
                       How do you feel?

He writes throughout, taking a scientific interest in what is happening

Sylvester   I've gone off this idea
                       Let's stop before we start
Crucible (*speaking*) Too late.
Sylvester   I think I've changed my mind now
                       I've had a change of heart
Crucible (*speaking*) Not yet but you will in a minute.

He pokes a thermometer into Sylvester's mouth and pulls it out again at once

                       Temperature falling
                       Fifty degrees
                       High perspiration
                       Weak at the knees

Sylvester collapses

There is a blood-curdling scream. Weird electronic music plays and the Lights flicker and change — strobe lighting is effective here

   Hyde enters and takes up a position behind Sylvester

Sylvester and Hyde move together in perfect unison, Hyde behind Sylvester, during the dialogue up to Sylvester's exit

   (*To Sylvester*) How are you feeling?
   (*To Hyde*)   Where is the pain?
   (*To Sylvester*) Try to describe it
   (*To Hyde*)   Try to explain
Sylvester } (*together*) Strange
Hyde   }   I feel strange
                              Pain
                              Oh the pain

During the following lines Sylvester "disappears" behind the lab. bench

Hyde   I've gone off this idea
                        Let's stop before we start
                        I think I've changed my mind now
                        I've had a change of heart

Crucible And that's not all. You've had a change of face, arms, legs and one or two other things. A few more moments of excruciating agony and the transformation will be complete but in the interests of science can you tell me please

(singing)   Where does it hurt you?
                        How is your head?
                        Answer me quickly
                        Before you drop dead.

Hyde clutches his head, screams and falls as if dead

Drat! (*He consults his formula*) I must have used too much rat poison. (*He scribbles on paper*)

Hyde stirs

But wait!

Hyde jumps up, flexes his muscles and feels his new body

Well do you still think this was a mistake?
Hyde No, I think I've changed my mind.
Crucible That too, yes. Here.

Crucible hands Hyde a mirror Hyde looks at himself and is delighted. Crucible takes the mirror Hyde snatches it back

Hyde Mr Crucible, you're a genius. This is unbelievable.
Crucible It works. It works.
Hyde Let's just see if the antidote works.
Crucible Antidote?
Hyde To turn me back.
Crucible Oh I see. You don't quite understand. There is no antidote. You just have to wait until it wears off.
Hyde How long will it last?
Crucible That I don't know. It could be hours or it could be weeks.
Hyde But, if it lasts weeks, people are going to notice that I'm missing
    That he's missing   That the other
Crucible Let's he honest, Jekyll. I shouldn't think anyone will care   that's if they even notice.
Hyde True   But what about
Crucible Don't worry. We'll sort everything out. The first thing we need is a new name for the new you. Any ideas?
Hyde Well   I   er   perhaps

There is a knock on the door

Crucible Hide!

Hyde Well I suppose that's as good a name as any.
Crucible (*aside*) He's still a half-wit. No—quickly—hide behind there. (*He indicates the bench*)

Hyde hides

Come in.

Miss Wrenplacket enters with Angela

Miss Wrenplacket Excuse me, Mr Crucible, I found Angela outside. She says she's waiting for Sylvester Jekyll. How long are you keeping him in for because she shouldn't wait if it's more than
Crucible I'm not keeping anyone in, as you see Miss Wrenplacket.
Miss Wrenplacket Well, Angela, really!
Angela I saw him come in here, Miss, and he hasn't come out.
Crucible It must have been one of the other rooms, dear

There is a noise behind the bench

Miss Wrenplacket What was that? Who's there? Come out at once.

Hyde emerges

Crucible Ah   yes   There you are   This is   er
Hyde Hyde.
Crucible (*looking round quickly*) Why?
Hyde My *name* is Hyde.
Crucible Oh Hyde   yes. Well, Hyde, have you cleaned up that mess you made?
Hyde Yes sir.
Crucible Well be off with you then.
Hyde Yes sir.

Hyde goes

Miss Wrenplacket Hyde. I've never seen him before. His clothes!
Crucible (*sitting and mopping his brow*) No   A new boy. Only arrived today.

Angela discovers Sylvester's school bag and books. She stands to one side

Miss Wrenplacket (*trying to make conversation*) Ah yes, there are so many aren't there? Ah well, the end of another day, Mr Crucible. Roll on Friday. (*She laughs and points to a stool*) May I?

There is no response. Crucible is looking very nervous. Miss Wrenplacket sits anyway, obviously all set for a chat. She inches her stool nearer to him. As she is about to speak, Crucible leaps up and heads for the door

Crucible Yes, well goodnight, Miss Wrenplacket. Time and tide, you know, time and tide.

Crucible leaves in a hurry

Miss Wrenplacket looks heartbroken. She rises and comes forward

During Miss Wrenplacket's song the lab. scene is removed and the Youth Club scene is set with the dancers and the band coming on stage

8. One Day

Miss Wrenplacket   I love him so, but I do nothing
I watch him go, but I say nothing
Why can't I say what I feel?
Why can I never reveal
My silent love?

One day, strength will come to me
One day, I will tell him he
Has my heart till the day that I die
One day!
One day, pigs will fly!

He looks at me and he sees nothing
My agony to him means nothing
But how will he ever know
If I can't bring myself to show
My silent love?

One day, I'll be brave enough
One day, screw my courage up
Steel my nerves and come out of my shell
One day!
There'll be snowballs in hell!

Angela comes forward

Miss
  Wrenplacket } *(together)* { I'd tell him I love him if I only dared
Angela   He might notice, might love, if he knew I
                          cared
                          One day, strength will come to me
                          One day, I will tell him he
                          Has my heart till the day that I die
                          One day!
                          One day pigs will fly!

Miss Wrenplacket and Angela leave

The scene is now the Youth Club. The band play the last few bars of "Let's Skit Together" As the song ends the dancers applaud and cheer

Ricky Let me introduce the members of the band. Here on guitar we have Billy Vandal.

Billy plays a few chords and the dancers applaud

And over here we have Everton Cool.

Everton plays a few notes and the dancers applaud

And on drums let's hear it for Kid Mozart.

Kid plays a few notes and the dancers applaud

Thank you. We're going to take a short break now and in the meantime there'll be a disco.

Loud taped music is heard. Four couples dance at the front of the stage

Hyde enters

Hyde walks slowly across the front of the stage past the couples. As each girl sees him she stops dancing and follows him. He sits down, with a girl either side of him. The four boys dance on until they notice they are alone. Then the boys talk in a group, deciding which one will tackle Hyde. One boy goes across to Hyde and they talk. Hyde gets up and excuses himself to the girls

Hyde and the boy exit

There is a pause

Hyde returns, alone

Hyde sits down with the girls. The three remaining boys talk together. One approaches Hyde. They talk. Hyde excuses himself to the girls

Hyde and the boy exit

There is a pause

Hyde returns alone

Hyde sits with the girls. The two remaining boys talk and a coin is tossed. The loser approaches Hyde. They talk. Hyde excuses himself to the girls

Hyde and the boy exit

There is a pause

Hyde returns alone

Hyde sits. The last boy stands for a long time wondering whether to tackle Hyde

He wanders off, finally, whistling nonchalantly

Hyde gets up and dances. He is soon surrounded by girls. The record ends

Keith approaches the band

Keith I hate discos. When are you playing again?
Everton Cool Ricky's not back yet.
Billy Vandal Anyone seen Ricky? Ricky!
Keith Come on.
Everton Cool We can't start without him. He won't be long.

Hyde jumps on stage

Hyde I'll give you a song.

There are cheers and applause

Billy Vandal No, mate. He won't be a minute.
Girl 1 Yeah. Let him sing.

There are cheers and cries of "Yeah"

Billy Vandal OK. What do you know?

A muttered discussion takes place between Hyde and the band

   Right then. One, two, three, four

The song which follows should be as loud, fast and horrible as possible. Hyde screams rather than sings

9. Love, Love, Nothing But Love

Hyde   Love, love, nothing but love
                     Love, love, love, still love
                     Love, love, love, still more
                     For oh love's bow
                     Shoots buck and doe
                     The shaft confounds
                     Not that it wounds
                     But tickles still the sore
                     These lovers cry, oh ho they die!
                     Yet that which seems the wound to kill
                     Doth turn "Oh ho!" to "Ha! ha! he!"
                     So dying love lives still

   Ricky enters during the song

                     Love, love, nothing but love
                     Love, love, nothing but love
                     Love, love, nothing but love
                     Love, love, nothing but love

The song is received with an ovation

Ricky (*to the Audience*) Cheek! My favourite song an' all. Music by yours
   truly. Lyrics by William Shakespeare (no rubbish). (*He jumps onto the
   stage*) Thanks mate. I'll take over now.
Hyde We'll talk about that later.
Ricky How do you mean?
Hyde It's a good band. I like it.
Ricky Yeah. Thanks.
Hyde That is, without you, I like it.
Ricky What's that supposed to mean?
Hyde The band just got a new singer.
Ricky (*laughing*) Will you tell him to get lost?

The band looks sheepish

   Well, go on. Tell him you've already got all the singers you need.

The band looks even more sheepish

Oh I see. I get the picture. (*To Hyde*) Could I have a word with you outside.

Ricky walks forward. Hyde shrugs and follows him

  I don't know who you are
Hyde Hyde.
Ricky (*looking over his shoulder in alarm*) Why?
Hyde My name is Hyde.
Ricky I don't care what your name is but if you think you can just walk in
here and take over my band then you've made one big mistake.
Hyde They seem quite happy about it and so did your audience.
Ricky Well I'm not.
Hyde That's understandable.
Ricky You

*Ricky jumps at Hyde. There is a brief fight. Hyde easily defeats Ricky who is
left lying on the floor*

Hyde goes back "inside"

  (*To the Audience*) I would have used me karate only I didn't want to hurt
him. (*He dusts himself down, winces with pain, and wipes away tears*) But
    "Let not women's weapons, water-drops,
    Stain my man's cheeks!
    I will have such revenges
    That all the world shall—I will do such things
    —What they are yet I know not—but they shall be
    The terrors of the earth. You think I'll weep;
    No, I'll not weep
    I have full cause of weeping but this heart
    Shall break into a hundred thousand flaws
    Or ere I'll weep."
(*He starts to go but turns*) Shakespeare! No rubbish!

  Ricky leaves

*Hyde is now with the band. During his song the Lights dim, leaving Hyde in a
single spotlight*

  Everyone slowly leaves the stage as Hyde comes forward for his song

10. All The Best Days Of My Life

Hyde All my life
    I've been pushed around and said
    Next time I'll fight but not yet
    In my life
    I very soon found instead
    That I was incurably "wet"

He gives a triumphant laugh, jumps from the stage and comes forward

Now I can have what I've been waiting for
I can have what I could never hope for before
The bad days, the sad days, the old days are gone
They'll be high days, blue sky days, my days from now on!
All the best days of my life
On their way
All the best days of my life
Start today
From now on the world can't get in my way
From now on they'll hear what I have to say
Because here they come, here they come
All the best days of my life
All the best days of my life

All my life
I've looked at the girls and said
I love each one that I see
In my life
I thought I'd always find instead
No girl that I want would want me

Now I can have what I've been waiting for
I can have what I could never hope for before
The bad days, the sad days, the old days are gone
They'll be high days, blue sky days, my days from now on!
All the best days of my life
On their way
All the best days of my life
Start today
From now on the world can't get in my way
From now on they'll hear what I have to say
Because here they come, here they come
All the best days of my life
All the best.days of my life

There is a Black-out

INTERVAL

ACT TWO

The scene is the Youth Club three weeks later The band starts to play and dancers mill about the stage

Inspector Ticket enters from the back of the auditorium, shouting for quiet

There is no response so Ticket blows his whistle. The band stops

Ticket Quiet! Stop that! Stop the performance at once! Nobody move! I have the building surrounded! (*He glares at the Audience, having now reached the stage. He waves his warrant card*) Detective Inspector Ticket. Scotland Yard. I think there's been foul play! I have reason to believe you can help us with our enquiries. I am investigating the disappearance of one Sylvester Jekyll, missing from his home for three weeks. Now I'd like you to take a look at this photograph. (*He produces a tiny photograph*) When did you last see this boy?

There is a pause

When did you last   Oh so you won't talk eh? This is typical. Typical of the response we get from the public nowadays. What has happened to the old spirit of co-operation upon which we could once rely? What has happened to the wonderful warm relationship between the British public and the friendly bobby? Perhaps I can shed some light

A spotlight comes up on Ticket

on the matter

11. Out On The Beat

(*singing*) Time was when the bobby enjoyed the respect
And the love of the people he'd serve and protect
Now it's sneer at the law, idolize Ronald Biggs
We used to be heroes but now we're called "pigs"!

Crime increases each year
But you've no need to fear
Just as long as we're here
Yeah
The police on the beat!

How long ago was it? It seems yesterday
"Your policemen are wonderful", tourists would say
Now each year the complaints and hostility grow
You seem to forget *we're* the good guys you know

Crime increases each year
But you've no need to fear
Just as long as we're here
Yeah
The police on the beat!

I read the newspapers and watch the TV
Police corruption, misconduct and brutality
To hear them you'd think we were all on a par
They don't seem quite sure who the criminals *are*

Crime increases each year
But you've no need to fear
Just as long as we're here
Yeah
The police on the beat!

(*Speaking*) Just a minute. Just a minute. Isn't that

*Ticket shields his eyes against the light and speaks to the follow spot operator
The music stops*

Can we have a light down here?

The light moves

No   over here a bit   Stop   that's it   I thought so. Look who it is.
How long have *you* been out? And over there

The light moves

That way   that lad over there. Thought I wouldn't recognize you, didn't
you? Record as long as your arm. Gentleman here.

The light moves

Stopped battering your wife have you? And what about this side?

The light moves

Here we are. Here we are. Coach party in from Strangeways. And look at
him.

The light moves

If ever anyone needed a short, sharp shock. About ten thousand volts
should do the trick. And there's an interesting face.

The light moves. Ticket pulls out a "Wanted" poster

Yes. Doesn't do him justice does it? What kind of audience *is* this?

The spot picks out members of the Audience during the following verse

The muggers, the flashers, the killers, the thugs
The vandals, the burglars, the pushers of drugs

With the dregs of society we deal every day
Well *you'd* be corrupted if *you* lived this way

As mob violence spreads
You rest safe in your beds
We'll be out smashin' heads
Yeah
The police on the beat!

Although it might appear police brutality's here
If you keep off the streets you have nothing to fear
Yes it's easy to tell by the screams from the cell
That the police are in charge and it's all going well

As mob violence spreads
You rest safe in your beds
We'll be out smashin' heads
Yeah
The police on the beat!

(*Shouting*) Where are those people I wanted to interview? Get them in here.

During the final chorus Annie, Bert, Angela, Hyde and Crucible march on and line up

As mob violence spreads
You rest safe in your beds
We'll be out smashin' heads
Yeah
The police on the beat!

Hyde and Crucible are arguing heatedly. Crucible hands Hyde a bottle

Crucible It's only a little.
Hyde What good's that?
Crucible It's a slow process. I'm working as fast as I can. And I've got other worries you know. Slasher's escaped.
Hyde Slasher?
Crucible You know, my creature, in the trunk. I usually keep him locked in there, when there are children about you know. He's very fond of children.
Hyde You don't mean   .?
Crucible Yes   it hasn't been fed today.
Hyde (*looking right and left and into the audience*) I expect it will turn up somewhere. But what about this policeman? I think he's suspicious. Why did he want *me* here?
Crucible Don't worry. Leave it to me. How could they ever suspect what's happened?
Ticket (*shouting*) Be quiet, you two! No talking! You stand at the end there! Right. I've read this note signed by your son which you say was pushed

through your letterbox on the day he disappeared. Now, I want a detailed description of the boy. You first, Mrs Jekyll. What was he like? (*He opens his notebook*)

Annie "Was"? "WAS"? WAAAAAAAAAAAAAAAAAAH!
Bert Shaddup woman!

Bert belts Annie. Ticket wallops Bert with a truncheon

Ticket Don't interfere with the witness! Well, madam, if you insist on being optimistic, what *is* he like?
Annie Well, he was a quiet boy.
Bert *You* said "was" then!

There is a pause

Annie Waaaaaaaaaaaaaaaaaaah!

Ticket wallops Bert again

Ticket Don't interrupt. You've got a lot to say for yourself. You tell me about him.
Bert (*dazed*) Dooh   er   ooh   ow.
Ticket (*hitting him again*) A comedian eh? We know how to deal with your kind at the Yard. Now, one at a time, tell me what sort of boy Sylvester w   er   is.

They all look at each other, unable to think of anything to say. Angela sobs

Well, did he have any distinguishing features?
Annie Well   er   no.
Angela Yes!
Bert None at all.
Angela He did!
Hyde He would never have stood out in a crowd.
Angela Head and shoulders!
Crucible I think I can give you what you want, Inspector. Sort of a verbal Identikit picture.
Ticket Exactly. Yes.
Crucible OK. Write this down.

Ticket starts writing in his notebook

12. Points Of View

Crucible	Weak and seedy
	Windy, wet and weedy
	Ugly
Angela	Lovely!
Crucible	Wasn't worth a light

Angela pulls Ticket to face her She points to his notebook and dictates. Throughout Hyde is pleased and surprised to hear what she has to say about his other self

Angela	Shy, but charming
	Timid, but disarming
	Gentle
Crucible	Mental
Angela	Thoughtful and polite

Ticket leaps forward and performs an eccentric crab-like dance sideways as he sings to the audience

Ticket	Looking for the real Sylvester
	Outer shell and inner man
	Trying to build up a picture
	Try to help me if you can

Ticket returns to the others

(*Speaking*) There are one or two inconsistencies here, you know.

			Which is ficti ↑
			Which description?
Angela	}	(*together*) {	Now I know I loved him true
Crucible			Oh he made me want to spew
Both			It depends on your point of view

Ticket	Looking for the real Sylvester
	Outer shell and inner man
	Trying to build up a picture
	Try to help me if you can

Crucible	Had no friends here
	Let his story end here
	I'd leave him
Angela	I love him
Crucible	Keep him out of sight

Angela	Handsome, wholesome
	Often sad and lonesome
	Lovesome
Crucible	Loathsome
Angela	Always does what's right

Ticket	Looking for the real Sylvester
	Want to know what made him tick
	Build a kind of mental picture
	Character identikit

(*Speaking*) I'm a bit confused. Your descriptions don't seem to tally.

			Which is fiction
			Which description?
Angela	}	(*together*) {	Now I know I loved him true
Crucible			Oh he made me want to spew

Both   It depends on your point of view

Hyde is spotlit to one side, listening with wonder and astonishment

Ticket, Bert and Annie all perform Ticket's eccentric dance as before

Ticket ⎫   ⎧ Looking for the real Sylvester
Bert   ⎬ *(together)*   ⎨ Want to know what made him tick
Annie   ⎭   ⎩ Build a kind of mental picture
                              ⎩ Character identikit

All freeze except Hyde who sings at first doubtfully, diffidently

Hyde   Free yourself, accept yourself
                                  Be yourself, respect yourself
                                  Don't feel sorry for yourself
                                  Ignore the rest, be more yourself

*He repeats the lines with more confidence. The others then come to life. Angela
and Crucible sing simultaneously*

Angela   Shy but charming   **Crucible**   Weak and seedy
             Timid but disarming   Windy, wet and weedy
             Gentle   Ugly
             Lovely   Mental
             Thoughtful and polite   Wasn't worth a light

Ticket ⎫   ⎧ Looking for the real Sylvester
Annie   ⎬ *(together)*   ⎨ Outer shell and inner man
Bert   ⎭   ⎩ Trying to build up a picture
                              ⎩ Try to help me if you can

Then all at the same time

Ticket ⎫   **Angela**   Handsome wholesome
Annie   ⎬ *(together)*   Often sad and lonesome
Bert   ⎭   Lovesome
    Looking for the real Sylvester   I love him
    Want to know what made him tick   Always does what's right
    Build a kind of mental picture
    Character identikit   **Crucible** Had no friends here
                                                         Let his story end here
                                                         I'd leave him
                                                         Loathsome
                                                         Keep him out of sight

All six come together for the final chorus

All   Which is fiction
                                  Which description?
                                  Now she knows she loves him true
Crucible   Oh he made me want to spew
                                  It depends on your point of view

All	Which is fiction
	Which description?
	Now she knows she loved him true
Crucible	Oh he made me want to spew
	It depends on your point of view
	It depends
	On your point
	Of view!

All exit singing "Looking for the real   ", except Hyde and Angela. Crucible calls "Slasher!" as he goes

Hyde approaches Angela. She snuffles into a handkerchief

Hyde Angela?
Angela Yes.
Hyde Hyde.
Angela (*alarmed*) Why?
Hyde My name is Hyde.
Angela Oh yeah, I know.
Hyde Er   listen   I was thinking   you doing anything tonight?
Angela Why?
Hyde Well you seem a bit upset. I thought you might need   er comforting.
Angela After all those terrible things you said about Sylvester. You've got a nerve. Get lost.

Angela kicks Hyde on the shin and leaves

Hyde hops around, stops, look after her, thinks

Hyde leaves

The scene is changed to the School Library. There are four tables and chairs and a large sign, made up of individually hung letters, saying "SILENCE"

Gail, Denise, Chris and Eddie enter

The four sit at separate tables. Each pulls out a magazine and turns to the problem page. They get out paper and pen and start to write

Gail Dear
Eddie Dear
Denise Dear
Chris Dear
Gail   Mary
Eddie   Marjorie
Denise   Lucy
Chris   Anna

13. Problem Page

Chris   I'm writing to your problem page
              Please help me

Gail	They say I'm going through a phase
	It could be
Eddie	That I have reached an awkward age
	But really
Denise	Life's not worth living nowadays
	I'm lonely

Girls enter and "Oooh" and "Aaah" behind the chorus

Chorus
All   Wanna girl (boy)
A hand to hold
Wanna girl (boy)
'Fore I'm too old
Wanna girl (boy)
Two lips to kiss
Wanna girl (boy)
Can't live like this

Each of the four stands to deliver his or her line

Eddie	Is it because of me pimples they don't like me?
Chris	Is it because I'm skinny I don't score?
Gail	Is it because I'm too fat?
Denise	Is it B.O., something like that?
All	Oh, I don't want to be lonely any more

Chorus

The girls now go to the "Silence" sign and remove the letters, bringing them to the front and using them to spell out the words in the following sections. The missing letters are on the backs of the originals

Chris	L is for my life that's not worth living
Gail	O is for my outlook which is bleak
Eddie	N ywhere I turn *E*verywhere I learn
Denise	Love is like a game of hide and seek
All	Y does it have to be me?
	Why do I have to be
	The ONLY one (*The letters spell "only"*)
	The LONELY one (*The letters spell "Lonely"*)

The four pull out hankies and wipe away tears

Eddie	Can it be because I can't make conversation?
Denise	Is it because they think that I'm a bore?
Chris	Is me character vile?
Gail	Maybe it's the way that I smile
All	Oh, I don't want to be lonely any more

Chorus

The "backing" girls leave

The four come forward smiling at their finished letters. They then lose all confidence, tear the letters in half and throw them on the floor They turn to leave

   Miss Wrenplacket enters and points to the mess on the floor, then exits

The four pick up their torn letters

   Gail and Denise leave

Eddie Hey Chris, what are you doing in the library?
Chris Writing a letter.
Eddie Me too. (*He waves his letter, then looks at it more closely*) Hang on. This isn't my letter.
Chris And this isn't mine.

Chris and Eddie swop letters

   Nor's this.
Eddie This one's signed "Denise"
Chris This one says "Gail"

They piece the letters together and read. They smile, finish reading and fold the letters away

Eddie What was in that one?
Chris Oh nothing. What was yours?
Eddie Only a load of rubbish.
Both Which way did they go?

They both laugh

Eddie This could be me big chance.
Chris It seems like   almost   sort of   fate like.
Eddie Yeah. (*He looks around on the floor*)
Chris What are you looking at?
Eddie Er   well   If we got their letters

They suddenly realize

Chris } (*together*) { They've got ours!
Eddie }

The two boys prepare to run after the girls

Chris } (*together,* { Hey girls   hang on there   Gail!   Denise!
Eddie } *as they go*) { Wait a minute.

Black-out

The scene changes to Hyde's "pad" There is a sofa and some kind of screen, behind which Sylvester is hiding

Hyde is carried on by a group of girls. He tries to free himself from their clutches

Hyde Girls. Girls. You must excuse me.

The girls refuse, shouting "No", "Why", etc.

Look at the time. I have to get changed. You know I'm singing at the school dance tonight.
Girls Oh no. Stay. Just a few more minutes. Let them wait. *etc.*
Hyde I'm sorry. I understand how you feel but really it's not fair for you to keep me all to yourselves, is it? You know in a way I envy you.

The girls cling to him, swaying gently as he sings

14. I Rule

Yes it must be great!
I wish I was in your shoes!
It must be wonderful to know a guy like me!
With me for your date
The one every girl would choose
I mean to say how lucky can you be?

Chorus
Did you ever dream
Of a boy, to bring you joy?
Your dream's come true
Did you ever dream
Of a love, sent from above?
I've come to you
I don't want to boast
I know it ain't cool
I may seem big headed
But the truth is — I rule

I know how you feel
You don't want to let me go
I can see how it's hard to tear yourselves away
Don't try to conceal
Your feelings — just let them show
If I were you then I'd feel the same way

He starts to repeat the chorus but falters, clutches his stomach, excuses himself and staggers behind the screen. From the other side Sylvester emerges. The dressing gown worn by Hyde is, of course, much too big for Sylvester Sylvester keeps his back to the girls

Girl 1 Are you all right?
Sylvester Yeah   it's nothing   just a cough.

As Girl 1 approaches Sylvester grabs a paper bag and puts it over his head

Girl 2 What are you doing? What's happened to your dressing gown?
Sylvester (*disguising his voice*) Don't worry. It's OK. Have you seen my coat? Where's my coat?

Girl 1 hands the coat to Sylvester

Girl 1 Here.

Sylvester gropes in the pocket, finds the bottle and pushes it under the paper bag. He groans and staggers behind the screen. Hyde re-emerges

Hyde Where was I?
Girl 3 Are you all right?
Hyde Am I all right. You haven't been listening. I'm terrific.

As Hyde finishes the song he dresses in his stage clothes

> I envy you all
> For finding a boy like me
> Tall, dark and handsome and built like Hercules
> You're having a ball
> And quite understandably
> Each part of me has been designed to please
>
> *Chorus*

Black-out

The scene changes to become a back alley. There is a brick wall, dustbins, piles of rubbish, etc.

Ricky enters, wearing jeans and a leather jacket. A gang of muggers gathers behind him

Ricky Did you miss me? I expect you've been wondering what happened to me after me humiliating defeat in the first act. Well, "If you have tears, prepare to shed them now." Still Shakespeare—no rubbish. This is the really sad part of the story. When I was thrown   when I *left* the band, it had a terrible effect on me. My whole character changed. I sold me Cliff Richard records, threw away me Boy Scout's woggle and turned to a life of crime.

Ricky joins the muggers

A little old lady totters on, carrying a handbag

The gang attacks her and tries to steal her handbag. She puts up a very good fight. There is an acrobatic chase around the stage. They finally overpower her and divide up the money in her bag

(*To the Audience*) It's not our fault we do this you know. I blame it on the decadent materialist substructure of our capitalist society meself. Innit lads?
Muggers Yeah.

15. Society

Mugger 1 You say that this country's seen better days
Mugger 2 And that we're just a part of a general malaise

Mugger 3   Well I don't understand what you mean by all that
Ricky   So get outta my way and get offa my back

               You want us to be good, to be quiet and behave
               Well there's time for all that when I'm in me grave
               We want life, we want kicks, we want girls, fame and wealth
Mugger 3   We want aeroplane glue on the National Health

               Chorus
All   Society
               Society
               What have you ever done for me?
               I hate you
               And you hate me
               We're all at war with society

There is an instrumental section during which a little girl enters sucking a lollipop. She is grabbed and thrown around in an alarming way. The muggers fight over the lollipop as she runs off crying

Mugger 1   It's youth unemployment you say is to blame
               "Give 'em jobs and the juvenile crime you'll contain"
Mugger 3   But what you don't include in your Job Training Schemes
               Are the sight of the blood and the sound of the screams

Ricky   You say that you want us to keep off the streets
               Give us football and discos like you give kids sweets
               We've got a new Youth Club it's your latest gift
Mugger 3   We'll burn the place down on November the Fifth

               Chorus

There is an instrumental section. A blind man complete with white stick enters. They go up to him politely and helpfully show him the way. They gently guide him towards the edge of the stage, grab his wallet and push him off

Mugger 2   You try to explain but you don't know the half
               It's a great mugging life and a great mugging laugh
Ricky   It's 'cos I'm inarticulate I'm dissolute
               I've a reticent tongue but an eloquent boot

Mugger 1   At the Saturday match we go on the rampage
               But it's only 'cos we're at a difficult age
Ricky   Remember when *you* talk of muggers and thugs
               That *we* are the victims – and *you* are the mugs!

               The Chorus is sung twice

During the chorus the muggers spray paint on the walls, swing from ropes, throw rubbish at the Audience, etc.

After the song the muggers hide as they hear Sylvester coming

Sylvester staggers in, wearing Hyde's stage suit with a long coat covering it, down to the ground

The muggers start to creep up on Sylvester

Sylvester It's worn off again. I must get to Crucible. There isn't much left. (*He takes out the bottle and is about to drink*)

The muggers grab Sylvester's arms and take his money

Hey, give me that!
Ricky Have this instead.

Ricky punches Sylvester in the stomach. The muggers drop him and start to go. Sylvester opens the bottle and drinks. He gets up, turns towards them and growls. They turn and laugh at him. The muggers surround Sylvester (to conceal his changeover to Hyde) and step back as Hyde leaps up. Weird noises and electronic music is heard as the muggers move towards Hyde

There is a Black-out. Pause

The Lights come up to reveal all the muggers in comic KO positions—upside down in dustbins, etc. Hyde picks up the empty bottle, turns it upside down, looks at his watch

Hyde exits

The Lights fade

When ready the Lights come up to reveal the Chemistry Lab.

Miss Wrenplacket enters, picks up bottles, looks at papers and drops a pile of them but picks them up hurriedly

Crucible enters and looks hopefully in the trunk but it is still empty

Miss Wrenplacket Oh Mr Crucible, you gave me quite a start.
Crucible I'm so sorry. Is there something I can do for you? (*He starts working*)
Miss Wrenplacket No   no   I was just passing and I thought I'd drop in for
Crucible Mmm?
Miss Wrenplacket Just to   er   . (*She is suddenly determined*) Mr Crucible, there's something I must say to you.
Crucible (*vaguely*) Yes?
Miss Wrenplacket Heaven knows what you'll think of me for saying this but I can't allow another day to go by without expressing the feelings that have been growing within me. They are powerful feelings, Mr Crucible, powerful feelings. I can't suppress them. Believe me I have tried. Oh how I have tried! But they will not be suppressed. For months I've refused to admit it to myself, for months I've tried, months of inner torment but it's no use. It's like a volcano within me – bubbling, bubbling, burning, burning, growing and multiplying itself until it can contain itself no longer. Today   today, Mr Crucible, I have erupted!

Crucible (*looking up*) Sorry. What did you say?
Miss Wrenplacket I have erupted!
Crucible Oh dear. I think I have some Alka-Seltzer somewhere.
Miss Wrenplacket No! No! Don't you understand?
Crucible Er
Miss Wrenplacket I'll put it to you simply. In three simple words. Three
   small words that have sounded through the ages. Three words Mr
   Crucible   (*She turns to look at him*)

Hyde rushes in

Hyde I need it   quickly.
Crucible That's four words. Oh it's you. Yes. Well it's been very nice talking
   to you, Miss Wrenplacket
Miss Wrenplacket You can call me .

Crucible pushes her "out" She comes forward

Crucible   but as you can see I'm rather busy.
Miss Wrenplacket But
Crucible Have a good weekend. See you on Monday. Goodnight.

8a. One Day

Miss Wrenplacket   I love him so but I do nothing
                        I watch him go but I say nothing
                        Why can't I say what I feel?
                        Why can I never reveal
                        My silent love?

Hyde and Crucible are in conversation at the bench

Crucible You haven't seen any sign of Slasher, have you?
Hyde What does he look like?
Crucible Well he's sort of (*he gestures*) and (*he gestures*). Hard to put it into
   words really.
Hyde (*looking at Miss Wrenplacket*) Hey, you know, I think she fancies you.
Crucible God forbid.
Hyde I've used all the potion. I need some more for tonight. You might as
   well give me another bottleful.
Crucible What makes you think she fancies me?
Miss Wrenplacket   He looks at me and he sees nothing
                        My agony to him means nothing
                        But how will he ever know
                        If I can't bring myself to show
                        My silent love?

Hyde (*shouting*) Whaddya mean there is none?
Crucible I'm working on it. (*He looks angrily through his papers*) What's
   happened to these?
Hyde I'm singing tonight. School dance.
Crucible They're all over the place. It's that half-witted woman.

Miss Wrenplacket   One day, strength will come to me
One day, I will tell him he
Has my heart till the day that I die
One day
One day pigs will fly!

Hyde What if it wears off? What am I going to do?
Crucible Go to the dance. I'll get it to you as soon as I can. (*He looks frantically through the papers*)
Hyde Well hurry up. I don't want to turn back into that little snivelling creep.

Hyde exits

Crucible What was she doing here? That woman wants locking up.
Miss Wrenplacket   One day, I'll be brave enough
One day, screw my courage up
Steel my nerves and come out of my shell
One day
There'll be snowballs in hell!

Miss Wrenplacket leaves

Crucible (*finding the right page*) Ah here we are. (*He picks up bowls, test tubes, etc.*) Where was I? Yes   yes . done that   Now what? Heat for twenty minutes at three hundred and fifty degrees fahrenheit or gas mark four until golden brown   ah the excitement of the experiment   the thrill of discovery! (*He pauses in his experiment and comes forward*) Hands up all the little boys and girls in the audience who want to be scientists when they grow up. Good. Now listen children

A rhythmic bubbling noise starts in time with the music

16. Science Can Be Fun

Chorus
Hear them bubble
Hear the potions bubble
See the test tubes
How they froth and run
Hear my story
Let it be a lesson
Let me tell you kiddies
Science can be fun

There is an explosion on the lab. bench

(*Speaking*) I wanted to be a scientist when I was your age too

The verses are half sung, half spoken in the manner of a music hall comic song

Ricky enters and crosses the stage

When that I was and a little tiny boy

Ricky Shakespeare—no rubbish.

Ricky exits

Crucible (*with a glare at Ricky*) I knew I had a scientific bent
    All chemistry sets I soon found were useless toys
    I much preferred my own experiment
    I heard that a cat when it falls from any height
    It lands upon its feet and thus survives
    While proving this untrue by our pussy's downward flight
    I also found it didn't have nine lives!

A cat falls from the roof at the appropriate moment, landing with a squeal and a thud. The RSPCA recommend the use of an imitation cat for this effect. Spoilsports

    Chorus

Crucible holds up the potion

    I hold here a symbol of the never-ending line
    Of products of our toil, our tears, our strife
    Yes, all the men of science from Nobel to Frankenstein
    Who have improved your quality of life
    From the men who brought you napalm bombs and ring-pull cans
    This potion, which took ten years to create
    Our science gave you mustard gas and non-stick frying pans
    Germ war and monosodium glutamate

    Chorus

Smoke starts to pour out of the lab. bench

    I meet success and failure with equal peace of mind
    I never let a setback set me back
    I just keep looking forward, all mistakes I leave behind
    With each defeat I launch a new attack
    It would take more than one failure to see my train derailed
    For science must achieve all science can
    Take Slasher (*he indicates the trunk*) an example, an experiment that failed
    My first attempt to build a Superman

A blood curdling roar is heard from the back of the auditorium. It is Slasher He is huge and hideous. Crucible shields his eyes against the lights

(*Speaking*) Slasher? Slasher, is that you? Everybody just sit very still. Don't panic. Perfectly still and you'll be quite safe. It's only children he goes for usually. Thank God there are no children here.

Slasher roars and grabs a (planted?) child from the audience, picks him up and runs towards the stage with him

Slasher! Put him down, Slasher! He's far too big. You couldn't possibly eat all of him, and it would be a terrible waste.

Slasher ignores Crucible

There are people starving in India you know! Give him to me. Come here.

Slasher has reached the stage. Crucible chases him round

Slasher runs off

Chomping noises are heard off. Some bones are thrown on. Crucible catches them and turns to the Audience

Some you win. Some you lose. But that's the great thing about science, isn't it? You go on. You don't give up. The thrill of the chase, the pursuit of perfection.

The Chorus is sung twice. Then there is smoke, fireworks, coloured lights and a HUGE explosion

Black-out

In the Black-out the backstage staff put out fires (!) and smelling salts are distributed amongst the Audience

The Lights come up on the School Dance. The band are finishing a song. The Dancers and Hyde are on stage

Hyde And now I'd like to dedicate this next song to our ex-singer, Ricky Fantasy. Ha, ha, ha. It's a song he wrote for the band and it's called "Shakespeare   "
All (*shouting*) NO RUBBISH!
Hyde Yeah.

17. Shakespeare—No Rubbish

Way back in history in Rome and in Greece
They saw plays wrote by Aeschylus and Sophocles
Although they weren't bad, they still gave them the bird
'Cos they knew which dramatist they'd have preferred

Chorus
All   Shakespeare—no rubbish
That's what the audience wanted to see
Shakespeare—no rubbish
Down through the centuries they all agree

Banners are produced with pictures of Shakespeare, slogans, etc. Everyone dances madly

Hyde Tomorrow and tomorrow and tomorrow again
There'll be queues for the works of this greatest of men
Plays will still come and go, absurd and sublime
But none shall outlive Shakespeare's powerful rhyme

Chorus

The best in this kind are but shadows, he said
But the life of his plays underestimated
Friends, Romans, countrymen lend me your ears
Yeah, it still gets a laugh after four hundred years

The Chorus is sung twice

During the second Chorus repeat Inspector Ticket climbs on stage, with Bert and Annie

Ticket All right, all right. Now just shut up and listen.

A guitar twangs. Ticket gives the guitarist a look

Thank you. Pay attention. This is the police. As you may know I have been investigating the disappearance of   er   of a member of this school namely   er

Annie Sylvester Jekyll.

Ticket Ah yes. Sylvester Jekyll. Now I want any information you can give me about the evening of October fifteenth last, the day Sylvester was last seen alive. I shall be interviewing you individually in a few moments but first Mrs Jekyll would like to speak to you all. (*He helps her up to the mike*)

Annie I just want to say that our son   well he wasn't much   nothing at all really   not like some you see   in fact he was always a bit of a disappointment to Bert and me   he was never

Ticket coughs significantly

Ticket What did you want to say to them?

Annie Well, all I meant to say was that he may not be the world's greatest son but   (*trying not to cry*)   I really miss him and if you can think of anything that might help us find him I   (*she collapses in tears*)

Ticket helps her down. Bert comforts her Hyde watches her walk away in anguish. He goes towards her but stops. Ticket notices this and approaches Hyde

Ticket Now then Hyde I've an idea you know something about all this. (*Aside*) If he be Hyde, I shall be seek!

Ticket motions Hyde to one side. They talk animatedly. Four girls, including Angela, are gathered in a group. They look at Ticket and Hyde

Girl 1 Look at that. Do you think he knows anything about Sylvester?
Girl 2 You know I knew there was something funny about him.
Girl 3 Do you reckon he's done him in?
Angela You've all changed your tunes. He was the greatest thing since (*latest teenage idol*) a few minutes ago.
Girl 2 Naw. I never really liked him.
Girl 1 Yeah. I mean I don't like boys that are sort of *too* good-looking really. Know what I mean?
Girl 3 Yeah. He's a big-head too, isn't he?
Girls 1 & 2 Yeah.

Angela All I want to know is what's happened to Sylvester. I hope he's all right.

Hyde leaves Ticket and joins the girls

Hyde Er   girls   I think I need your help here. Sherlock Holmes seems to think I had something to do with this Sylvester business. Now you could get me out of trouble here. How about you telling him I was with you that night.

The girls look at each other

What do you say, girls? Just to help me out because it's getting a bit sticky with this inspector.

The girls stare at him

It's only a little white lie.

The girls split up and leave him

Thanks a lot, girls. (*To the band*) Hey fellers. Here a minute.

The band members come over to Hyde

Listen lads. Do us a favour. Will you tell this copper that I was rehearsing with you when this Sylvester kid disappeared? He's got it into his head that I had something to do with it.

Billy Vandal Well, I don't know.

Kid Mozart Isn't that perjury or something?

Hyde Come on, lads. If he arrests me, what'll happen to the band?

Everton Cool Well I've been meaning to talk to you about that.

Kid Mozart Yeah we're not sure we like the way things have been going since you took over.

Hyde Eh, fellers. This isn't the time to be arguing about the band. I'm going to get thrown in gaol in a minute. Now come on. You know I had nothing to do with this.

The band walks off

(*Following them*) Lads   eh, lads   come on!

Hyde walks off

Ticket comes forward holding two pieces of paper

Ticket This note left by Jekyll and the statement Hyde has just written There's a rather singular resemblance; the two hands are in many points identical; only differently sloped   curious.

Ticket follows Hyde, deep in thought

Gail and Denise enter, showing each other their letters

Denise I didn't look at it till I got home.

Gail Me neither.

Denise I couldn't believe it.

Gail Me neither.
Denise Who did you say wrote yours?
Gail Me neither   oh   Chris.
Denise Mine was Eddie.
Gail Eh Denise. (*Laughing*) Look at this bit 'ere. (*She points to a section*)

Denise laughs. She takes Gail's letter

Denise This is the best bit in mine. Here. (*She points to the letter*)

They laugh. Gail shrieks with laughter and takes the letter

   Eddie and Chris enter

   (*Seeing them*) Eh, Gail. Here they are.

Gail shrieks with laughter at something in the letter Denise waves Gail's letter at Eddie and Chris

   (*Reading*) Dear Anna

Chris and Eddie hold up letters

Eddie (*reading*) Dear Lucy

Gail shrieks with laughter

Chris (*reading*) Dear Mary

Gail stops suddenly

Gail Here give me that.
Chris Not till I get mine back.
Gail Give it him, Denise.
Denise Not till I get mine.
Gail Well who's got yours?
Denise (*pointing at Eddie*) He has.
Gail Give it her.
Eddie Not till I get mine.
Gail Well who's got yours?
Eddie I don't know
Denise You have, Gail.
Gail What?
Denise If you give him that, he'll give me that and then I'll give this one to him and you can have yours.

Gail thinks carefully about this

Gail Come again.
Chris It's simple. Look.

Chris takes the letters, passing them to the others. They all look at their new letters

Gail This isn't mine.
Denise Now I've got yours, Gail.

Eddie You've mixed them up, you idiot. Here. (*He transfers the letters to their proper owners*)
Denise That's it.
Chris Great.
Eddie Listen, Denise, I was wonderin' about what you wrote

Eddie and Denise walk off together talking and laughing

Gail Eh, do you really do what you said in that letter?
Chris (*embarrassed*) Er . . yeah   listen, I think I can help you with what you said about   you know

Gail looks puzzled. Chris points at her letter

Here. Look.

Gail reads, looks at Chris and shrieks with laughter

Gail and Chris walk off together

Ticket brings Hyde forward

Hyde Supposing it were as you suppose, supposing Jekyll to have been well   murdered. What could induce the murderer to stay? That won't hold water; it doesn't commend itself to reason.
Ticket I'm afraid I shall have to ask you to accompany me to the station. I must warn you that
Hyde Oh   oh   AH   (*He clutches his head and starts to sway*)   the potion   it's wearing off. Has anyone seen Crucible? I must see Crucible. Aaaaaaaaaaaaaaaaaaah!

He falls to the floor Everyone gathers around. Then with a gasp of horror everyone steps back to reveal both Jekyll and Hyde lying on the floor They get up slowly, staring at each other They move like reflected images in a mirror All the others stand gaping

Hyde Jekyll!

18. It's My Life

Who invited you to this party?
You think you can gatecrash my life?
You had your chance and you blew it
Leave this to someone who knows how to do it

Chorus
I'm letting you know
That you'll have to go
'Cos you're in *my* way
Get out of *my* way
Don't care what *they* say
Don't care what *you* say
It's just not *your* day
It's *my* life, *my* play

Sylvester   You won't be the cuckoo in my nest
             You think you can push me aside
             The fight is on and I'll win it
             This is *my* life and you have no part in it

Both   There is no room for us both here
             I'm staying so you'll have to go
             Both Jekyll and Hyde I may be
             But I don't think much of your version of me

  Chorus

 Crucible rushes on

Crucible Hyde, I have it here What?

Crucible holds out the bottle. Jekyll tries to grab it but Hyde gets it first

Sylvester NO!!
Hyde Now Jekyll, you awkward weedy little insect, I can be rid of you for good.

He holds up the bottle and looks around at the horrified spectators

  but I will not drink. (*He throws the bottle high and away*)

Miss Wrenplacket catches it, looks at it curiously, opens it and takes a sip

 Miss Wrenplacket leaves, holding her head

Sylvester But but why? You cannot exist without it.
Hyde I cannot exist? I have never existed. I am just a dream. You dreamt me.
 I am what you wanted to be strong popular all of it I *we*
 enjoyed it for a while but we have learned

Hyde sinks to his knees becoming weak. Sylvester kneels beside him

Sylvester What? What have we learned? I've learned something here but I
 don't know what it is!
Hyde The things you wanted – the things I had my strength not
 important (*He is failing fast. He gasps for breath*) What matters is
 what's inside a person. Don't try to be someone else, Sylvester. You don't
 want to be like me. Be yourself. Respect yourself Well, life has been
 pleasant I liked it I used to like it

 There is smoke and Hyde disappears

Sylvester gets up. Angela rushes up and throws her arms around him

Angela Sylvester! I thought you were dead. Mrs Jekyll!

 Bert and Annie enter

Annie embraces Sylvester and cries

Bert By heck. This is going to cost us.

Annie Bert, whatever do you mean?
Bert Well he'll be wanting his bedroom back, won't he? We shall have to give the lodger notice.
Annie Bert! Really!
Bert Well all I'm saying is, "Is he worth twenty-five pounds a week?"
Annie BERT!

Annie belts Bert with her handbag and pushes him out

Crucible (*to Sylvester*) Jekyll, I think I owe you an apology.
Sylvester No, sir.
Crucible Yes, Jekyll. The whole idea was madness. I'm just an old fool.
Sylvester Oh no, you're not.
All Oh yes, he is.
Crucible The only important difference is not between strong and weak, beautiful and ugly, intelligent and stupid, it's between good and bad, kind and cruel, feeling and unfeeling and   what he said   what you said was right. You must be yourself, respect yourself.

19. Be Yourself

(*Singing*)   Don't let them tell you you're hopeless
                          Don't listen when they attack
                          Don't let them make you unhappy
                          Or long for what you lack

                          Tell them if they're dissatisfied
                          With your brains, your strength, your looks
                          The only supermen they'll find
                          Are in the comic books

All   It's no good to daydream or wish on a star
                          Pretending you're someone else won't get you far
                          Tell them all though it might make you unpopular
                          That they'll have to put up with you just as you are
                          Free yourself, accept yourself
                          Be yourself, respect yourself
                          Don't feel sorry for yourself
                          Ignore the rest, be more yourself
                          Free yourself, accept yourself
                          Be yourself, respect yourself
                          Don't feel sorry for yourself
                          Ignore the rest, be more yourself

Gail/Chris/   It really doesn't matter if
Eddie/Denise   You're weak, thick, ugly too
                          Forget your shortcomings but don't
                          Forget that you are you

You cannot choose the way you look
Can't change the way you're made
But what you *do is* up to you
Stand firm and unafraid

Ricky enters and addresses the Audience. He reads haltingly from a paper

Ricky   Our play has come to its conclusion
And brought an end to your confusion
Here was merriment in profusion
We hope you liked our brief illusion
And did not think it an intrusion
Now your applause we won't refusion

Crucible (*quickly*) Shakespeare?
Ricky (*tearing paper*) No. Rubbish.
Sylvester One thing has been worrying me, sir.
Crucible What's that?
Sylvester What happened to the potion?
Crucible I've an idea I saw Miss Wrenplacket with it.
Ricky You don't think?
Crucible She wouldn't, would she?
Eddie She would. Look.

Miss Wrenplacket enters, transformed. She wears a low-cut dress with a split skirt. Her hair hangs down. She has a rose in her teeth. She approaches Crucible

Crucible Miss Wrenplacket! Steady, Miss Wrenplacket!

She reaches him, grabs him and kisses him passionately

Miss Wrenplacket Eustace!
Crucible Guinevere!

She carries him off

All   It's no good to daydream or wish on a star
Pretending you're someone else won't get you far
Tell them all, though it might make you unpopular
That they'll have to put up with you just as you are
Free yourself, accept yourself
Be yourself, respect yourself
Don't feel sorry for yourself
Ignore the rest, be more yourself
Free yourself, accept yourself
Be yourself, respect yourself
Don't feel sorry for yourself
Ignore the rest, be more yourself
You can't fake it
You can make it
Try and see what you can do

> When you bring out the best in you
> You can't fake it
> You can make it
> Try and see what you can do
> When you bring out the best in you
> When you bring out the best in you

Black-out

CURTAIN

www.ingramcontent.com/pod-product-compliance
Lightning Source LLC
LaVergne TN
LVHW051806080426
835511LV00019B/3418